HUMAN BODY ANIMAL BODIES

HEALTHY BODIES

Izzi Howell

WAYLAND
www.waylandbooks.co.uk

First published in Great Britain in 2017 by Wayland
ISBN: 978 1 5263 0678 4
10 9 8 7 6 5 4 3 2 1

Wayland
An imprint of Hachette Children's Group
Part of Hodder & Stoughton
Carmelite House
50 Victoria Embankment
London EC4Y 0DZ

An Hachette UK Company
www.hachette.co.uk
www.hachettechildrens.co.uk

Produced for Wayland by
White-Thomson Publishing Ltd
www.wtpub.co.uk
Editor: Izzi Howell
Design: Clare Nicholas

Picture credits:
Getty: avid_creative 4tl, MikeLane45 9br, Andry5 11b, Wavetop 17c; Shutterstock: Javier Brosch *cover* t, Poznyakov *cover* b, Jacek Chabraszewski *title page* and 15tr, Shevs 4tr, Vishnevskiy Vasily 4bl, VaLiza 4br, Monkey Business Images 5t, tomkawila 5c, Serg Salivon 5bl, Mandy Godbehear 5br, karelnoppe 6, AlinaMD 7tl, Scisetti Alfio 7tr, Robyn Mackenzie 7cl, Rafa Irusta 7cr, multiart 7b, Johan Swanepoel 8, Tomas Mikl 9t, Olha Insight 9bl, Maxim Blinkov 10, Or_Flash 11t, Hung Chung Chih 12, Filipe Frazao 13t, Alexander Cher 13bl, antoni halim 13br, Samuel Borges Photography 14tl, Sergiy Bykhunenko 14tr, DMS Foto 14b, Duplass 15tl, Eduard Kyslynskyy 15b, Sergiy Bykhunenko 16, Alexey Seafarer 17c, Cat Downie 17b, ostill 18t, Anurak Pongpatimet 18c, effe45 18b, Gelpi 19t, jeep2499 19b, kdshutterman 20t, PolinaBright 20b, didesign021 21t, 135pixels 21b.

All design elements from Shutterstock.

The author, Izzi Howell, is a writer and editor specialising in children's educational publishing.

Contents

Healthy bodies

Humans and animals feel good when they are healthy.

When we are healthy, we are strong and have lots of energy.

an ant

a dog

We need to do these things to stay healthy.

eat

a chicken

drink water

If we stay healthy, we may live for a long time.

keep clean

a cat

keep warm

a tiger

sleep

Diet

Most humans are omnivores. We eat many types of food, including meat and vegetables.

What is the word for a person that doesn't eat meat?

omnivore: someone or something that eats meat and plants

Humans need to eat a balanced diet to stay healthy. A balanced diet includes different types of food.

lots of fruit and vegetables

lots of grains and cereals

some meat and fish

some milk and cheese

a small amount of butter and oil

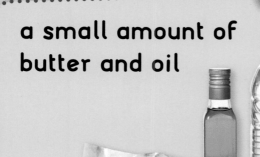

Animal diets

Animals have to eat the right type of food to stay healthy.

Some animals only eat meat. They are called carnivores.

a fish

Crocodiles are carnivores. They eat fish and other animals.

Find out the name of a carnivore that lives on land.

Herbivores are animals that only eat plants.

Sheep are herbivores. They eat grass and other plants.

Some animals are omnivores. They eat meat and plants.

Blackbirds are omnivores. They eat worms and berries.

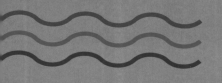

Water

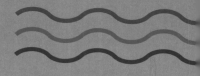

Humans and animals need to drink water to keep their body working. We also get some water from the food we eat.

Water is the best drink for our body.

Animals drink water from rivers or lakes.

zebras

Animals that live in dry places get water by eating plants.

a camel

Munch

While we sleep, our body rests and grows. Sleeping gives us energy for the day ahead.

Children need to sleep for around ten hours a day.

Zzzz

a koala

Some animals sleep in different positions.

in a tree

upside down

a bat

a flamingo

standing up, on one leg

Exercise

Doing exercise keeps our heart healthy.
We need to stretch and move to stay flexible.

dancing

kicking

Animals are
always moving.
They do lots of
exercise in their
normal lives.

This eagle
flaps its
wings to
fly around.

flexible: able to bend easily

catching

jumping

This frog
jumps to
move around.

How do
fish move?

Keeping warm

Being too hot or too cold can make humans and animals ill. Humans change their clothes so that they are the right temperature.

These children are wearing clothes that keep them warm.

Which clothes do people wear to keep cool in hot weather?

16

Animals warm up or cool down in other ways.

a dog

cool

panting

a polar bear

growing thick fur

warm

sitting on a hot rock

a lizard

warm

Keeping clean

Keeping clean helps humans and animals to stay healthy. We keep clean by ...

... brushing our teeth

... brushing our hair

... washing our body.

Animals need to keep their skin, fur or feathers clean. They clean away dirt and insects.

Some animals clean themselves.

a kingfisher

Other animals clean each other.

rhesus monkeys

Feeling ill

Most humans and animals fall ill from time to time, even if they have a healthy life. Sometimes we catch diseases, such as a cold.

a cat

Sometimes we cut or hurt our body.

We get better by resting and taking care of ourselves.

Sometimes, we need help from the doctor or vet to be healthy again.

the doctor

a horse

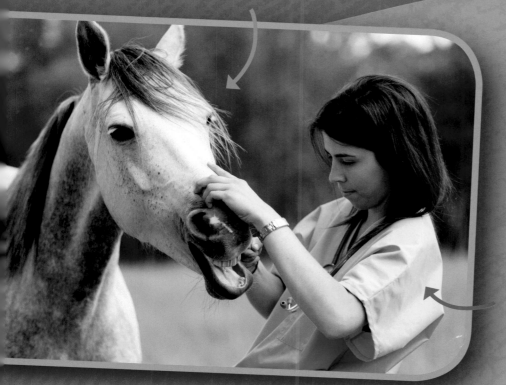

Vets help animals to get better.

the vet

Human and animal classification

Mammals

bat
camel
cat
dog

human
koala
polar bear
rhesus monkey
sheep

tiger
zebra

Birds

blackbird
chicken
eagle

flamingo
kingfisher

Amphibians

frog

Minibeasts

ant

Humans and animals need to do these things to stay healthy:

Eat
Drink water
Sleep
Move
Keep warm
Keep clean

Reptiles

crocodile

lizard

Index

Answers

p6 – Vegetarian
p8 – Lions, tigers and many more
p15 – By moving their fins
p16 – Shorts, t-shirts, dresses, skirts

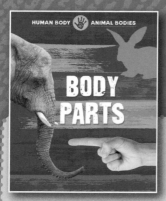

978 1 5263 0676 0

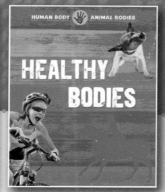

978 1 5263 0678 4

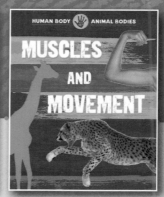

978 1 5263 0680 7

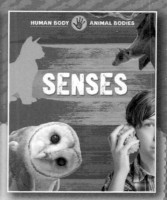

978 1 5263 0682 1

BODY PARTS

Human and animal bodies
Head
Neck
Skin
Hair and fur
Arms, wings and fins
Hands
Legs
Feet
Human and animal classification

HEALTHY BODIES

Healthy bodies
Diet
Animal diets
Water
Sleeping
Exercise
Keeping warm
Keeping clean
Feeling ill
Human and animal classification

MUSCLES AND MOVEMENT

Skeleton
Muscles
Exoskeletons
Walking
Running
Jumping
Swimming
Flying
Special movement
Human and animal movement

SENSES

What are senses?
Sight
Looking around
Hearing
Taste
Different tastes
Touch
Smell
Special senses
Human and animal senses

WAYLAND
www.waylandbooks.co.uk